BOOK ONE

# The Alfred d'Auberge Piano Course

MY NAME is .....Danny.....................................................

MY TEACHER'S NAME is .....Miss Julie.....................................
215-932-8277

*Illustrated by* ERNEST KURT BARTH

# GETTING ACQUAINTED WITH MUSIC...

# NOTES

Musical sounds are indicated by symbols called notes. Their time length is shown by their color, (white or black) and by stems and flags attached to the note:

etc.

# THE STAFF

The notes are named after the first seven letters of the alphabet, endlessly repeated to include the entire range of musical sound. The name and sound of the note is indicated by its position on five horizontal lines, and the spaces between, called the staff.

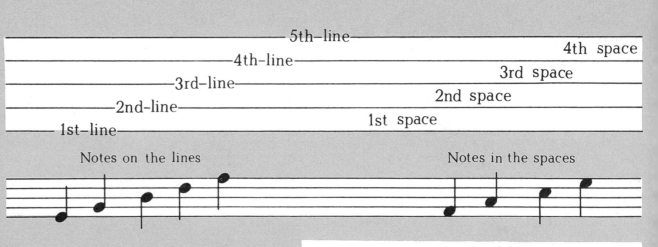

5th-line

4th-line

3rd-line

2nd-line

1st-line

4th space

3rd space

2nd space

1st space

Notes on the lines

Notes in the spaces

Every note on the staff has its own special place on the

# KEYBOARD

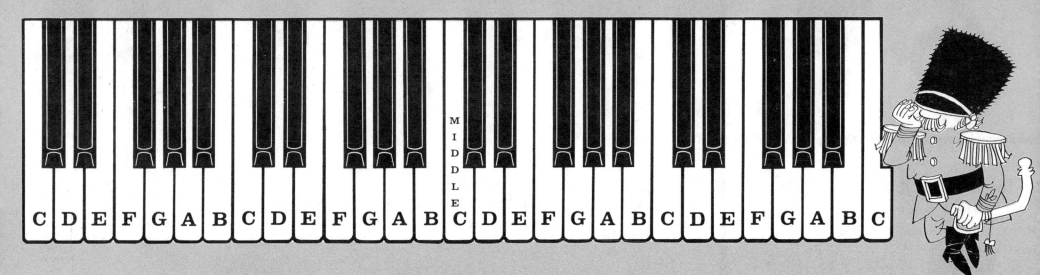

# MEASURES

Music is divided into equal parts called measures.
A bar line divides one measure from another.

bar line           bar line           bar line

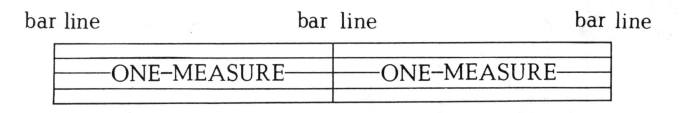

3

**Treble Clef** means play the notes with the right hand.

The thumb is the first finger.

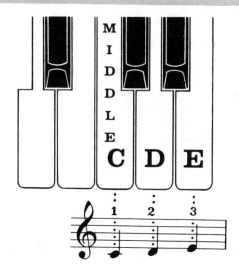

RIGHT HAND

# LET'S PLAY WITH CDE

(For right hand alone)

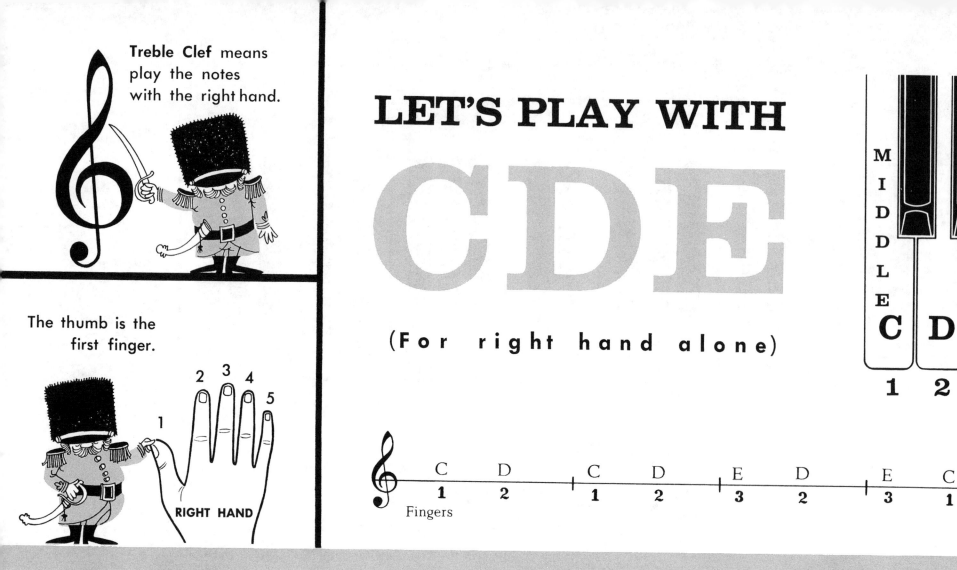

MIDDLE
C D E
1 2 3

C D | C D | E D | E C
1 2 | 1 2 | 3 2 | 3 1
Fingers

MIDDLE
C D E
1 2 3

## The same melody in notes

Fingers
1 2 3

C D C D E D E C

Sing the names of the notes as you play.

# The Animal Fair

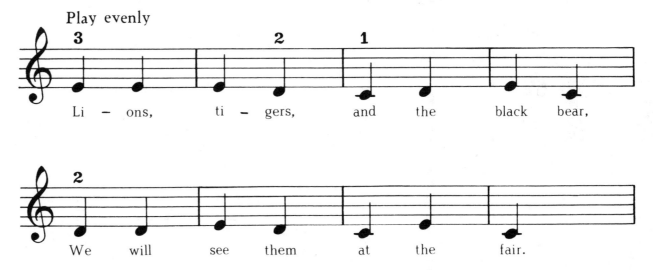

Play evenly

Li — ons, ti - gers, and the black bear,

We will see them at the fair.

5

**Bass Clef** means play the notes with the left hand.

The thumb is the 1st finger.

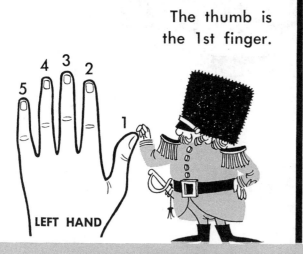

LEFT HAND

# LET'S PLAY WITH
# ABC

(For left hand alone)

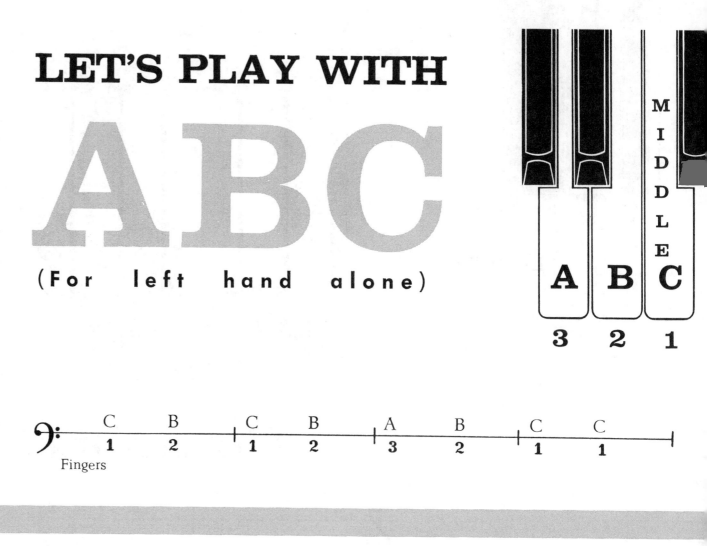

MIDDLE

A B C

3 2 1

𝄢 | C   B | C   B | A   B | C   C |
    1   2   1   2   3   2   1   1

Fingers

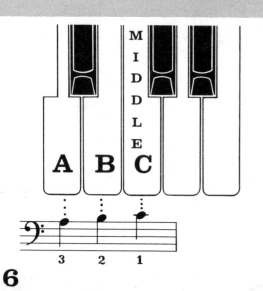

MIDDLE

A B C

𝄢
3  2  1

## The same melody in notes

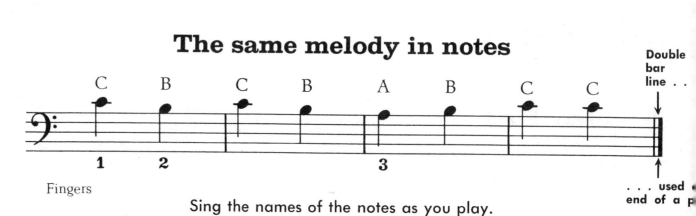

C   B   C   B   A   B   C   C

𝄢
Fingers   1       2               3

Double bar line . .

. . . used end of a p

Sing the names of the notes as you play.

6

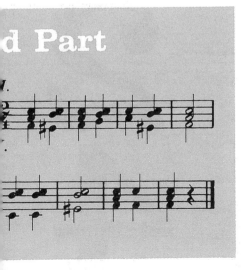

# At Our House

At our house we all watch T V,

There's so much we like to see.

Count: **1** 2 **1** 2

QUARTER NOTE ONE BEAT

HALF NOTE TWO BEATS

Count: **1** 2 **1** 2

## THE TIME SIGNATURE

At the beginning of every piece there are two numbers, called the time signature. The time signature tells us the number of beats to each note and each measure.

The top number tells how many beats in each measure.

The bottom number tells us that a Quarter Note has one beat.

**8**

# Three Blind Mice

Right hand staff joined by the bracket to the left hand staff.

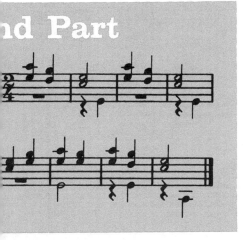

Three    blind    mice,    Two - four    time,

Half note gets two beats

Mice    can't    count    but    we    do    fine.

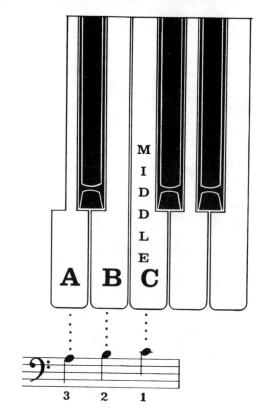

# Hallowe'en Space Witch

2nd Part

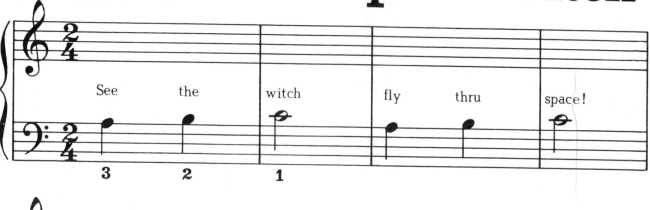

See the witch fly thru space!

3 2 1

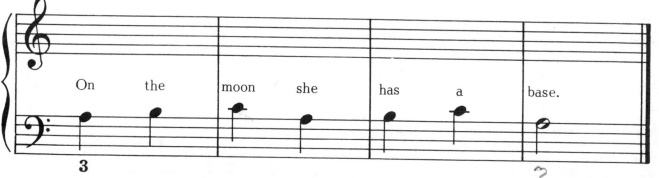

On the moon she has a base.

3

# WRITING NOTES

**WHOLE NOTES**  ○  Draw an oval.

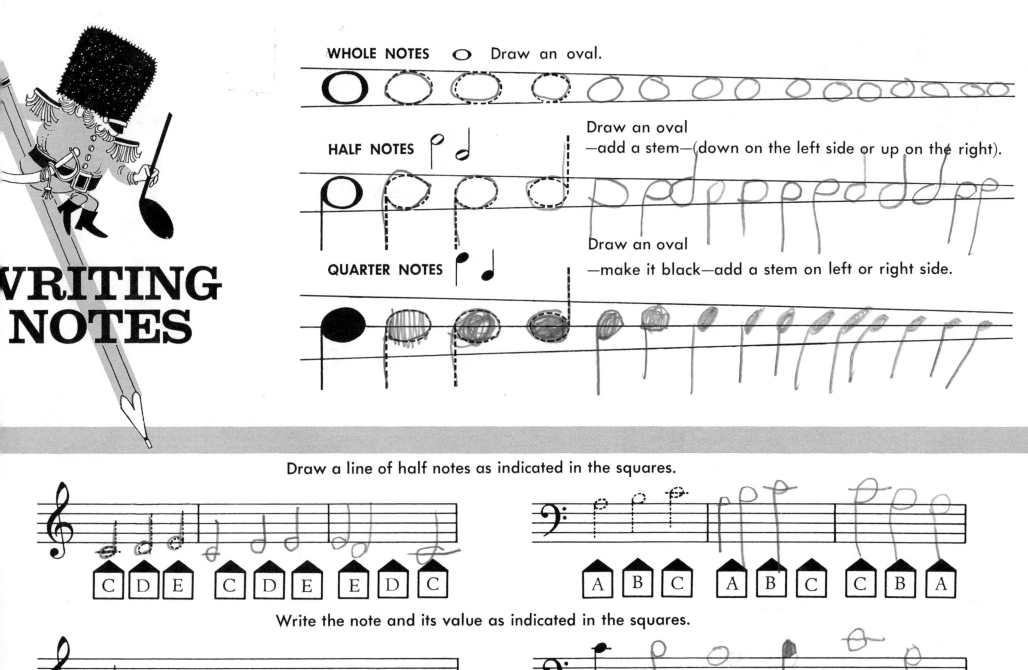

**HALF NOTES**   Draw an oval
—add a stem—(down on the left side or up on the right).

**QUARTER NOTES**  Draw an oval
—make it black—add a stem on left or right side.

Draw a line of half notes as indicated in the squares.

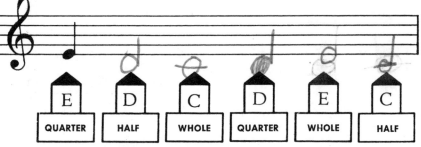

Write the note and its value as indicated in the squares.

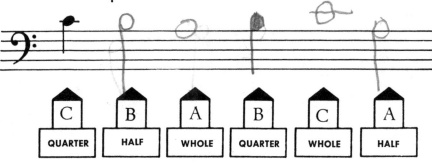

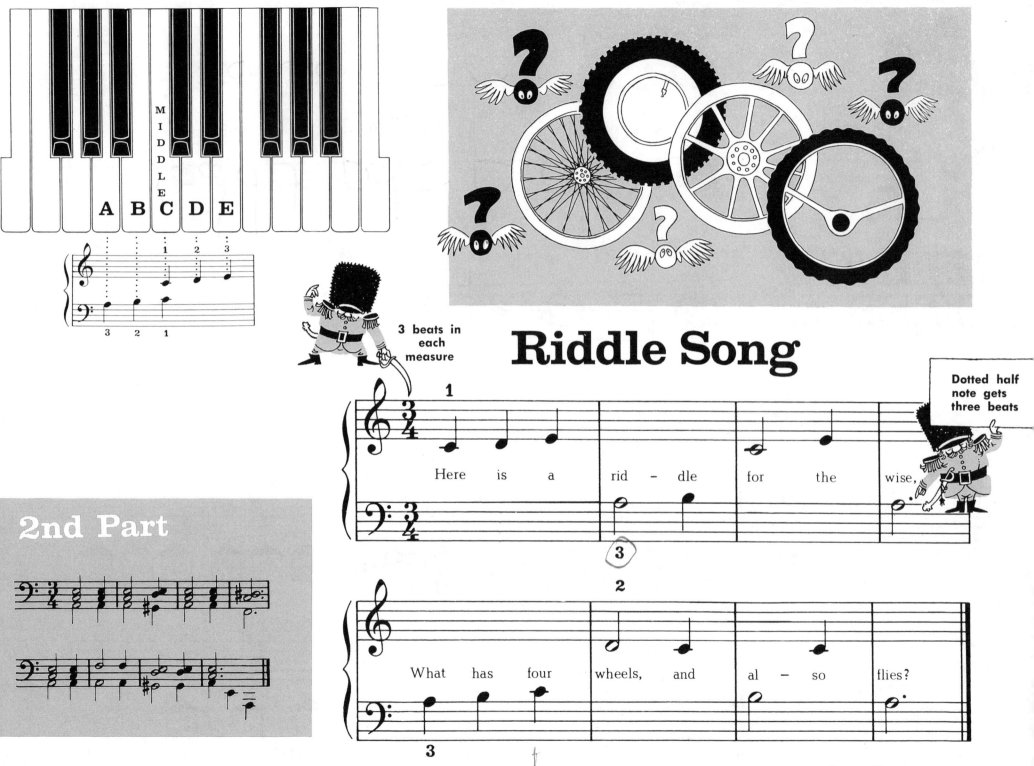

# Riddle Song

3 beats in each measure

Dotted half note gets three beats

**2nd Part**

Here is a rid – dle for the wise,

What has four wheels, and al – so flies?

Answer: A garbage truck.

# Willy The Whale

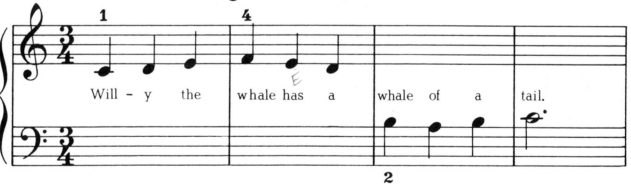

Will - y the whale has a whale of a tail.

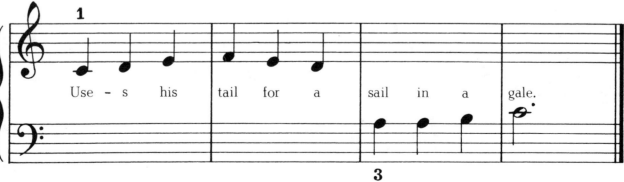

Use - s his tail for a sail in a gale.

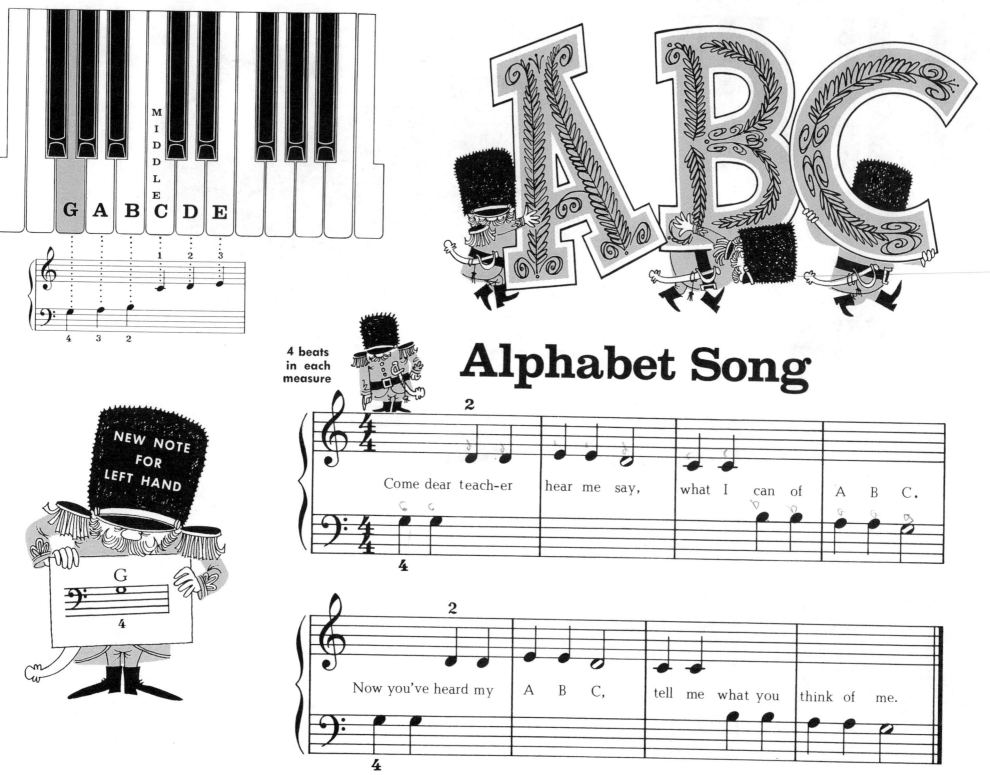

# Alphabet Song

**4 beats in each measure**

*Come dear teach-er hear me say, what I can of A B C.*

*Now you've heard my A B C, tell me what you think of me.*

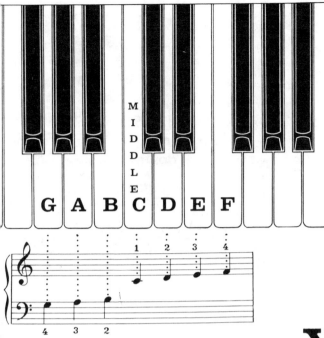

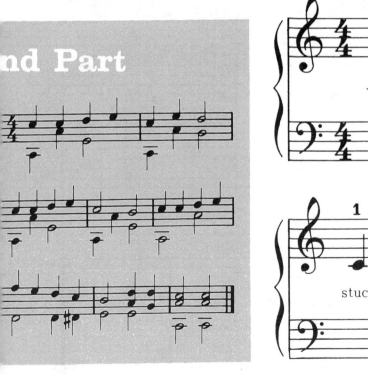

**nd Part**

# Yankee Doodle

Yan - kee Doo - dle went to town a - rid - ing on a po - ny, he

stuck a feath - er in his hat and called it mac - a - ro - ni.

# FUN WITH MIDDLE C

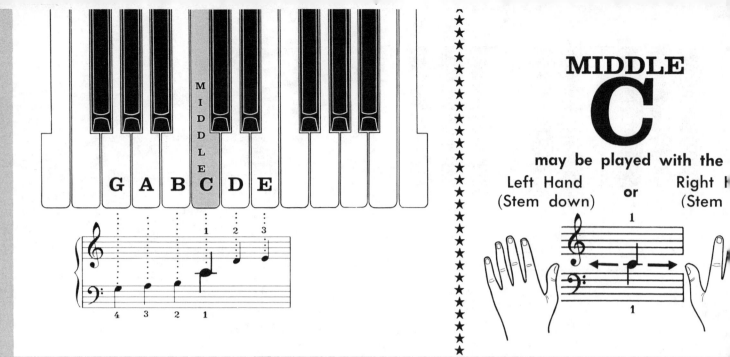

G A B C D E

## MIDDLE C

may be played with the

Left Hand          or          Right Hand
(Stem down)                    (Stem up)

# Chimes Of Westminster

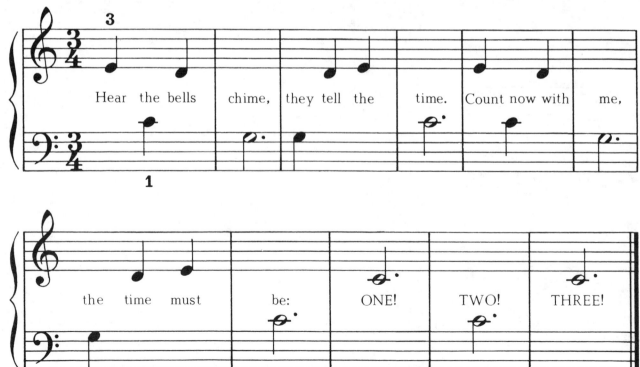

Hear the bells | chime, they tell the | time. | Count now with | me,

the time must | be: | ONE! | TWO! | THREE!

If you can reach the pedals, press down the **Damper Pedal** and keep it down throughout the piece. It will make a beautiful "Chimes" effect.

**16**

MIDDLE

G A B C D E F G

NEW NOTE
FOR
RIGHT HAND

nd Part

# The Bridge At Avignon

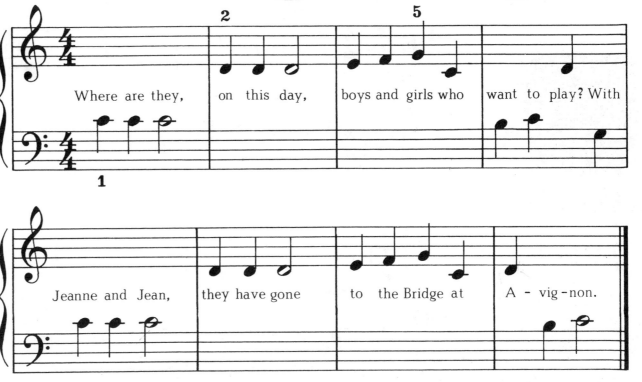

Where are they, on this day, boys and girls who want to play? With

Jeanne and Jean, they have gone to the Bridge at A - vig - non.

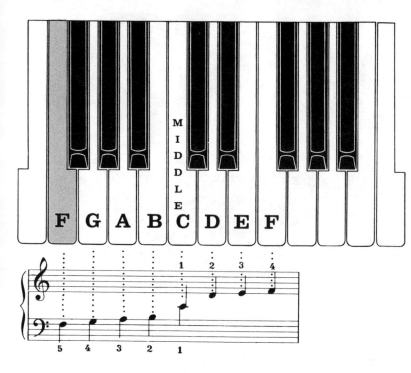

# Nonsense Song

NEW NOTE FOR LEFT HAND

Owls are whist-ling a sweet tune, To a square, pur-ple moon.

And a Span-ish Jag-u-ar, Sings up-on his gui-tar.

# The Big Parade

Come, boys and girls to the Big Pa — rade. There's

flags and there's march-ing while the mu — sic's played.

19

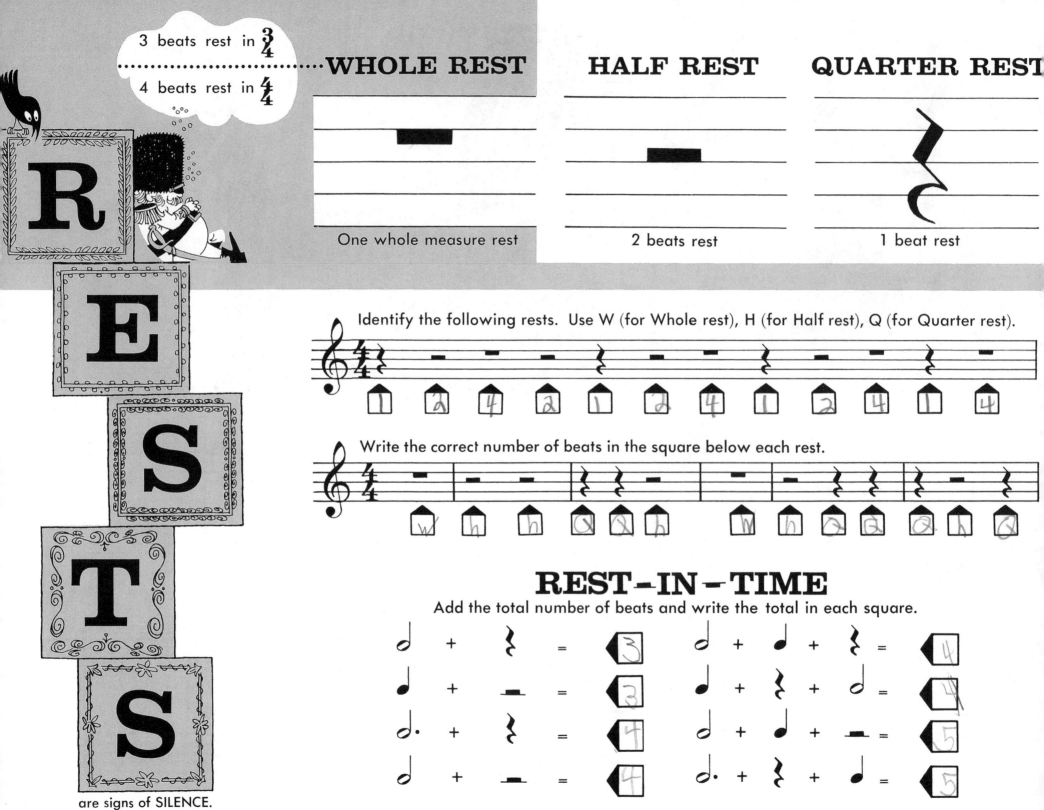

3 beats rest in 3/4
4 beats rest in 4/4

# R E S T S

are signs of SILENCE.

## WHOLE REST
One whole measure rest

## HALF REST
2 beats rest

## QUARTER REST
1 beat rest

Identify the following rests. Use W (for Whole rest), H (for Half rest), Q (for Quarter rest).

| 1 | 2 | 4 | 2 | 1 | 2 | 4 | 1 | 2 | 4 | 1 | 4 |

Write the correct number of beats in the square below each rest.

| W | h | h | Q | Q | h | W | h | Q | Q | Q | h | Q |

## REST-IN-TIME
Add the total number of beats and write the total in each square.

♩ + 𝄽 = 3     ♩ + ♩ + 𝄽 = 4

♩ + ▬ = 3     ♩ + 𝄽 + ♩ = 4

♩. + 𝄽 = 4     ♩ + ♩ + ▬ = 5

♩ + ▬ = 4     ♩. + 𝄽 + ♩ = 5

# Sing Tu Yoo

5 G
5 E
2 D
2 B
3 A

I am Chi-nese and my name is Sing Tu Yoo, I play

an-cient Chi-nese song and play it ver-y good, too;

sing it ver-y good, too, when I sing to you.

**The Whole Note gets 4 beats**

nd Part

# TIED NOTES

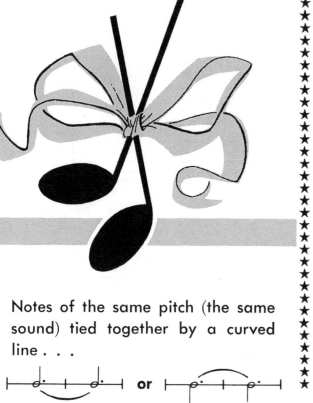

Notes of the same pitch (the same sound) tied together by a curved line . . .

. . . are TIED NOTES. Do not strike the 2nd note, "tie" its beats to the 1st note.

# Down In The Valley

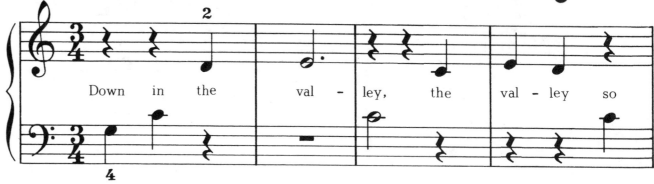

Down in the val - ley, the val - ley so

low. Hang your head o -

Tied Notes

ver, hear the winds blow.

**Two hands together !**

# Love Somebody

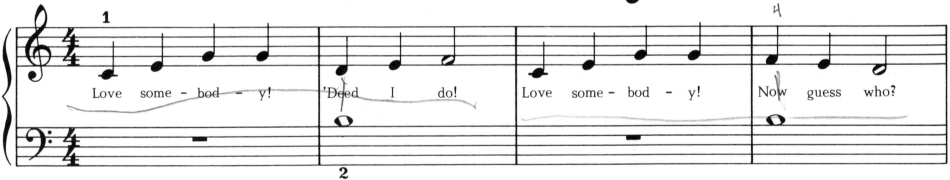

Love some-bod-y! 'Deed I do! Love some-bod-y! Now guess who?

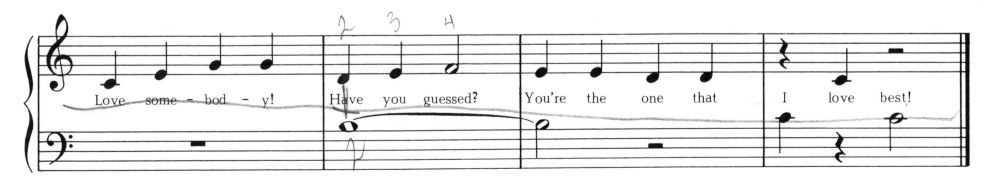

Love some-bod-y! Have you guessed? You're the one that I love best!

# INCOMPLETE MEASURES

Every piece does not begin on the first beat. Some songs begin with an incomplete measure, called the UPBEAT, or PICKUP. If the upbeat is one beat, the last measure will have only two beats in $\frac{3}{4}$

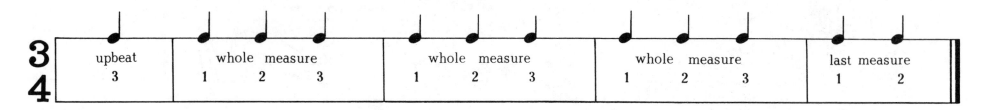

# On Top Of Old Smoky

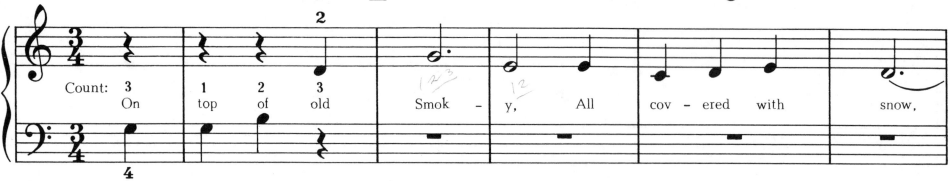

Count:    3        1      2      3                             All    cov - ered  with      snow,
          On      top    of    old        Smok  -  y,

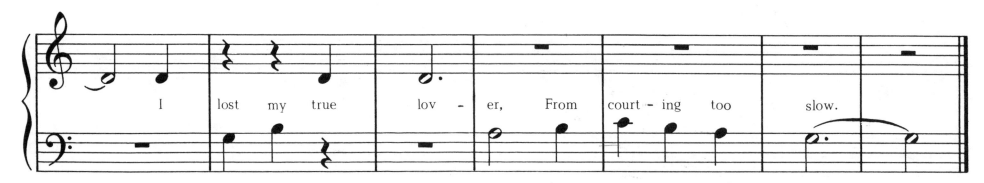

          I      lost   my    true        lov - er,  From  court - ing  too      slow.

**Two beat pick-up**

# Oh! Won't We Have A Jolly Time

Oh! won't we have a jol – ly time, Oh! won't we have a jol – ly time! Su –

Count: 3  4

san – na, put the ket – tle on, we'll all take tea.

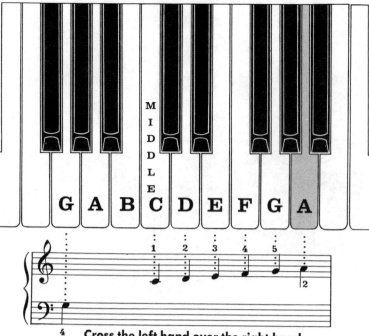

Cross the left hand over the right hand to play this new A. When the left hand plays the Treble (higher) notes, they are written in the Treble Clef.

# Pop! Goes The Weasel

Oh all a - round the Mul - ber - ry bush, the mon - key chased the wea -

sel! The mon - key thought 'twas all in fun, Pop! goes the wea - sel.

New position for Right Hand.

# Robin Hood

First Finger on D

We love to go a - rob - bin' with Rob - in Hood. We rob 'em with Ro - bin, but

give it to the poor of Sher-wood, We will go a - rob - bin' with Ro - bin Hood.

New position for Left Hand, and new note E.

## 2nd Part

# The Big Bass Drum

Oh I love the big Bass Drum, when the mu - sic goes boom!

Fourth finger on F

boom! With a rum-a-tum, a - tum, Oh I love the big Bass Drum.

Cross the left hand over the right to play this new C

MIDDLE C D E F G A B C

# Ride The Roller Coaster

# EIGHTH NOTES

Eighth notes are the black notes with a flag added to the stem

♪ ♪ or ♩ ♩

Two or more eighth notes are written

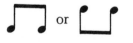 or ⌐⌐

To count eighth notes, we divide each beat into two parts, calling the 2nd part "and."

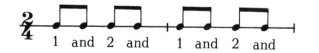

# Time To Get Up

C
The same
as 4/4

# Party Song

Count: **3**    and

This ⌢ is a hold sign (Fermata).  Hold the note longer.

# Barcarolle from "The Tales of Hoffmann"

Offenbach

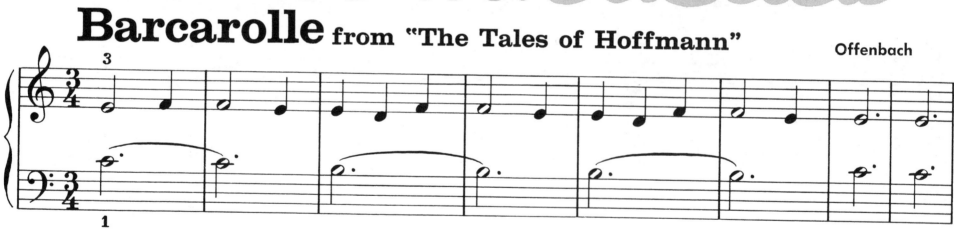

# Nick, Nack, Paddy Wack

This old man, | he played one, | He played nick, nack, on my drum, With a

Thumb on C

nick, nack, paddy whack, | give a dog a bone, | This old man came | roll -ing home.

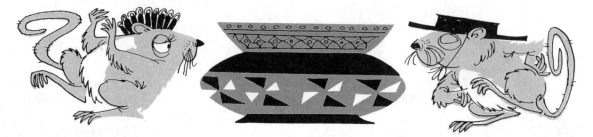

# Mexican Hand-Clapping Song

## A staccato dot

above or below a note means
to play the note short and crisp.

### 2nd Part

# Hop, Hop, Hop

Hop, hop, hop! We will nev-er stop! Where it's smooth and where it's ston-y,

In **4** the whole rest gets 2 beats

Trot a-long, my lit-tle pon-y. We will nev-er stop! When we go hop, hop!

# Jingle Bells

New Note **B** for Right Hand

Jin-gle bells, Jin-gle bells, Jin-gle all the way! Oh what fun it is to ride a one horse o-pen sleigh!

Jin-gle bells, Jin-gle bells, Jin-gle all the way! Oh what fun it is to ride a one horse o-pen sleigh!

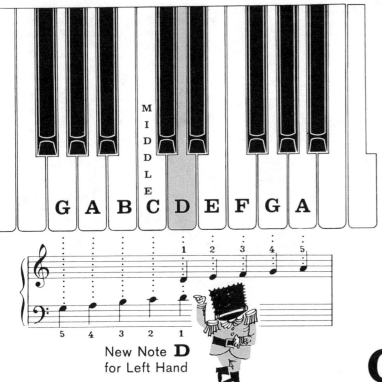

New Note **D**
for Left Hand

# Clementine

In a cav - ern, in a can - yon, Ex - ca - va - ting for a mine, Dwelt a

min - er, for - ty - nin - er, And his daugh - ter Clem - en - tine.

ten-shun!

Both hands are in TREBLE clef.

Cross the left hand over to play these two notes

# Swiss Song

# 10 Little Indians

1 lit – tle, 2 lit – tle, 3 lit – tle In – dians, 4 lit – tle, 5 lit – tle, 6 lit – tle In – dians,

7 lit – tle, 8 lit – tle, 9 lit – tle, In – dians, 10 lit – tle In – dian boys.

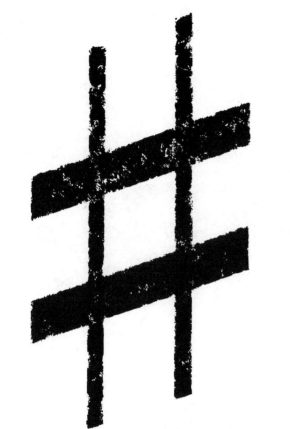

# The sharp sign

The sharp sign ♯ means to play the next key to the right, whether black or white. In this piece, the sharp is placed in front of F, which means you must play ........ **F♯**

instead of ......

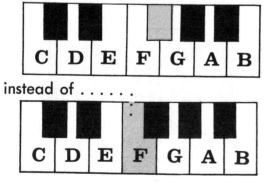

**40**

# Village Polka

The ♯ effects every other note on the same line or space in the same measure.

# Sour Wood Mountain

When there is a sharp sign placed after the clef
(called the Key Signature)
the sharp is placed on the F line
means that all F's are to be played sharp
throughout the piece.

Chick-ens are crowing on Sour Wood Mountain, Ho do do-ing doodle dum day.

So man-y girls, I just can-not count 'em, Ho do do-ing doodle dum day.

## The flat sign

The flat sign ♭ means to play the next key to the left, whether black or white. In this piece, the flat is placed in front of B,

which means you must play **B**♭

instead of . . . . . . . . . . . . . . . . .

# Little Brown Jug

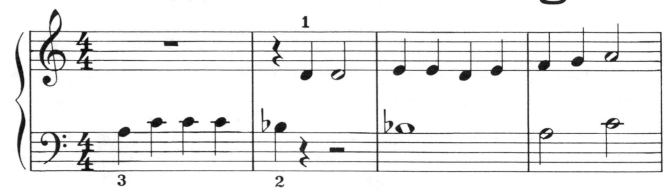

The ♭ effects every other note on the same line or space in the same measure.

# Old MacDonald Had A Farm

there is a flat sign placed after the clef
(called the Key Signature)
the flat is placed on the B line..........
and means that all the B's are to be
played flat throughout the piece.

Old Mac Don-ald had a farm, E I E I O! And

on that farm he had a duck, E I E I O!

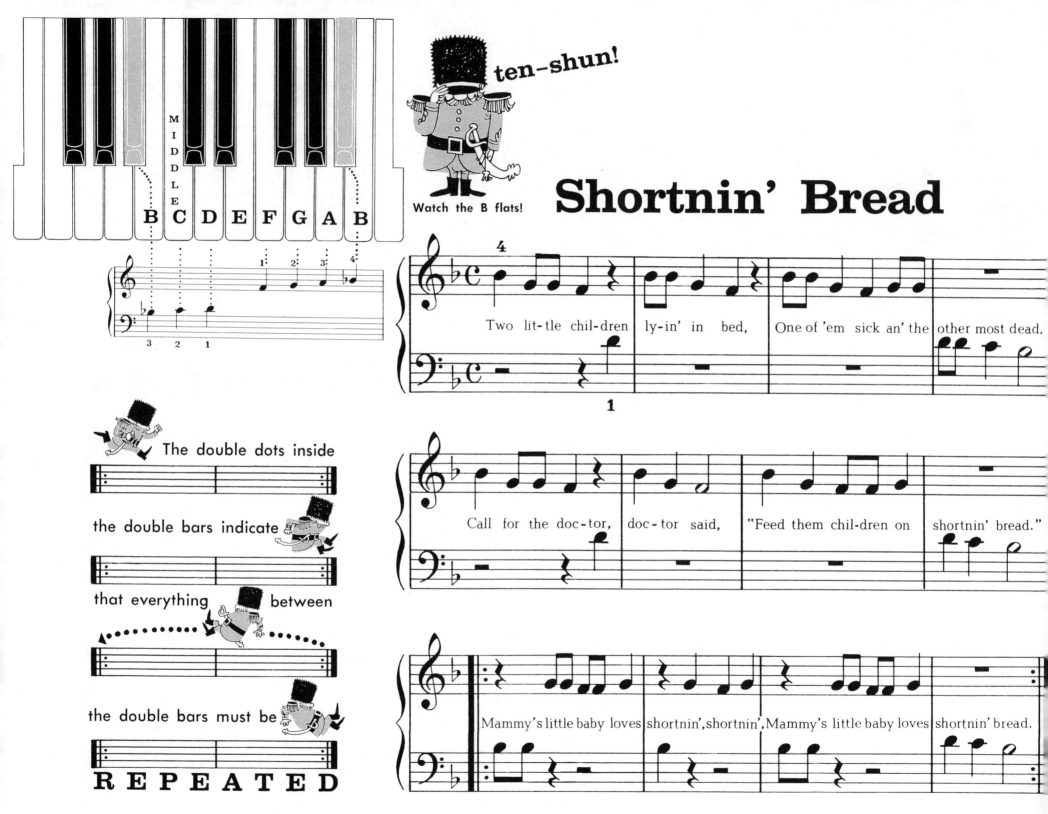

ten-shun!

Watch the B flats!

# Shortnin' Bread

The double dots inside

the double bars indicate

that everything between

the double bars must be

R E P E A T E D

Two lit-tle chil-dren ly-in' in bed, One of 'em sick an' the other most dead.

Call for the doc-tor, doc-tor said, "Feed them chil-dren on shortnin' bread."

Mammy's little baby loves shortnin', shortnin', Mammy's little baby loves shortnin' bread.

New position
for Left Hand,
and new
note C.

# Musette

J. S. Bach

# Chopsticks

1. The two clefs used in piano music are the _____ and _____ clefs.

2. Write the number of beats each note receives.

           ____   ____   ____   ____

3. Write the names of the following notes.

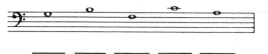

   ____    ____    ____    ____    ____

4. If the upbeat is one beat in ¾, the last measure will have _____ beats.

5. Write the names of the following notes.

   ____    ____    ____    ____    ____

6. The time signature 𝄴 is the same as ____.

7. If the upbeat is one beat in 4/4, the last measure will have _____ beats.

8. This symbol ⌢ is called a _____ or _____.

9. When two notes are connected by a curved line ⌢ or ‿, they are called _____ notes.

10. Add the correct time signature to each line.

**Q U I Z**

11. Below each rest, write the number of beats it should receive.

12. This ♯ is a _____ sign. It means to play the nearest note to the _____.

13. In 4/4 time there are _____ beats in each measure. In the measures below, add the rest signs that will give each measure the correct number of beats.

14. This ♭ is a _____ sign. It means to play the nearest note to the _____.

15. This 𝄞♯ is a key signature. The ♯ means that all _____ must be played _____.

16. To count 8th notes, we divide each beat into _____ parts, calling the 2nd part _____.

17. This 𝄞♭ is a key signature. The ♭ means that all _____ must be played _____.

18. On the staff below, draw the treble and bass clefs.

19. Fill in each measure with notes or rests to give each measure the correct number of beats.

20. The following piece should have one sharp in the Key Signature. Draw the correct sharp.

# Certificate of Promotion

## This certifies that

_____

has mastered and perfected

Book 1 of the ALFRED d'AUBERGE PIANO COURSE

and is hereby promoted into

Book 2 of the ALFRED d'AUBERGE PIANO COURSE

Teacher_____

Date_____